Staying
in Your Lane

COUPLE EDITION

DEMETRIA HIGH

WESTBOW
PRESS®
A DIVISION OF THOMAS NELSON
& ZONDERVAN

WestBow Press books may be ordered through booksellers or by contacting:

WestBow Press
A Division of Thomas Nelson & Zondervan
1663 Liberty Drive
Bloomington, IN 47403
www.westbowpress.com
844-714-3454

ISBN: 978-1-6642-8051-9 (sc)
ISBN: 978-1-6642-8050-2 (e)

Library of Congress Control Number: 2022918882

Print information available on the last page.

WestBow Press rev. date: 11/09/2022

Contents

Relationships vary, and not all are the same. However, principles and techniques can be applied in totality regardless of the differences so the relationship can bloom. As each of you embark on the reading of this devotional together, allow yourselves to learn and incorporate those principles and techniques for the growth of your relationship. *Staying in Your Lane* will help achieve those goals.

~ Clarence

It is important to know that every relationship starts, blooms, grows, and changes. Each of these stages requires us to revisit, review, and readjust our relationship every now and then. Never assume that the other person is all right, and never remain quiet about not being all right. *Staying in Your Lane* will help to balance those specific areas.

~Demetria

In Loving Memory
This devotional is dedicated to the memory of my late husband,
Clarence High, Jr., who collaborated with me to ensure that the
assignment God gave us for this book, and the vision for couples
and relationships as a whole, were fulfilled. Although God made
a decision to bring him home to be with Him before its release,
he is very much a part of this moment. In his words given to
so many of us, "Be Strong. Remember you have standards."

Forever Loved,
Your wife and Family
#BeStrong

Daily Reconnection

In today's world both men and women work outside of the home, which can add pressures to a marriage. These pressures come from having been disconnected from each other all day. This disconnection separates you from each other's presence, which is why when you come back home after a long time apart, you reconnect.

The Cambridge English Dictionary gives this meaning of *reconnection*: "To join or be joined with something else again after becoming separated." This means that something has become separated, untied from, or loosed away from something else. When you become physically untied by the busyness of the day, it is important to retie spiritually. Keep in mind that this is a reconnecting moment, which means a disconnection has occurred. Be careful not to remain disconnected too long.

The hustle and bustle of life can draw you away from reconnecting without you realizing it. Set aside time to come back together again. How? Before you start dinner, before you wash a load of clothes, before you call your family, before you turn on the television, before you _____ (fill in the blank), do one or more of these things.

- Sit down with your mate;
- Lay your head on his shoulder;
- Lay your head in her lap;

- Kiss him on the cheek;
- Kiss her on the forehead;
- Hug his neck; or
- Hold her hand—do whatever it takes.

Then inhale, exhale, inhale again, and exhale again. Now smile and tell your partner, "I missed you today!"

That is how you reconnect!

Go Touch It

"Wow! How beautiful their grass looks. We have dirt patches and weeds all in our yard. Why can't our yard look like theirs?"

These are statements from some couples who view other couples as having their ducks in a row and doing well. They show love to each other publicly and do not mind being affectionate for all the world to see. They are the "ideal" couple—or are they?

It is very important to be careful not to measure and compare other relationships with yours. As much as it may seem like they have it together all the time, remember that every couple has issues. As much as their grass looks greener, we challenge you to *go and touch it!* You will find that it is artificial! That's right. They have been watering artificial grass, and you have been admiring it. Their artificial grass gives the impression that there will never be arguments, there will never be disagreements, there will never be times one of them wants to turn and walk away, there will never be tears shed, blah, blah, blah. It costs to keep your yard green. It requires work to keep your yard green. Likewise, it costs to keep your relationship growing and glowing, and it requires joint work to keep it growing and glowing. Everyone has ups and downs in their relationships. Work through those ups and downs—do not camouflage them.

Couple Time Reading

How beautiful you are, my darling, How beautiful you are! Your eyes are like doves. How handsome you are, my beloved, And so pleasant! Indeed, our couch is luxuriant!

—Song of Solomon 1:15–16 (NASB)

Help Me with Me

It is easy for us to help others, but what about when we need help? We are not talking about help with doing something or buying something, but about self-help. In what areas do you need help with yourself? Do you know that when you are better, it makes your relationship better?

One of the hardest things for men to do is to ask for help, especially from their mates. However, God said that it was not good for man to be alone, so He formed a helpmeet. It is like God was putting a specific person in place to help meet his (the man) needs. God knew that one of the hardest things for a man is to ask for help. Why? Because he has a hard time dealing with himself. Women can be reluctant in asking for help because they have a tendency to be territorial and feel no one can do things like they can do them. A woman can be too proud to include anyone in how she feels or thinks. She smiles on the outside and appears to be happy, but that is not always the case.

Both need help with each other. Pride can stop you from doing so, but that is not what you want in your relationship. Ladies, he is your ministry. He will always need you because that is how God designed it. However, he does not need you going against him. He needs you to have his back. Gentlemen, she is your ministry. She will always need you to help her, not by fixing things all the time but by listening to her. She was designed as a suitable helper. This word *helper* comes from the

Hebrew word *ezer*, which means "strong power." She is your strength when you are weak. You are her strength when she is weak.

It is important that each of you help each other with each other. That is what will give the relationship strength.

Wedding Versus Marriage

As the man in the relationship, it is important to realize that the woman you are about to marry has thought about getting married her whole life. She has planned for her fairytale wedding and taken notes on specifics since she was a little girl. The details have been worked out. All you are preparing for is to select the tuxedo and show up at the altar.

A wedding happens in one day but takes months to prepare for, in most cases. However, a marriage is for as long as you both shall live, and there has not been any preparation for it. It begins one second after the wedding ends—when the flowers and decorations have been taken down, the food has been eaten, the dancing has ceased, all the guests are gone, and the wedding is no more. A wedding ceremony, in all honesty, takes ten to fifteen minutes; *a marriage takes a lifetime to master.*

Never get so caught up in the wedding that you do not think about the commitment in the marriage. A wedding is an event. A marriage is a lifestyle change.

> So they are no longer two, but one flesh. Therefore,
>
> What God has joined together, let no one separate.
> —Matthew 19:6 (NIV)

You Give Me Butterflies

Do you remember how giggly and silly you were with each other when you started dating? Or maybe you stayed up all night holding the phone to your ear until you fell asleep, only to wake up with the phone still to your ear, having listened to each other breathe all night. Maybe you experienced thinking about that person throughout the day, and it caused you to feel butterflies in your stomach. We call those the goofy, happy moments. So here's a question: when was the last time you had a butterfly moment in your relationship? When was the last time you had a goofy, happy moment? Or have you let moths take the place of the butterflies?

One very important thing for you to remember is the thing you do that gives your spouse butterflies. These are the things that make your mate smile, that cause her to give you that sexy look, and that cause him to wink at you every time you pass by. You need to learn what those things are and keep doing them. Do not stop after a couple of months of winning your mate and then think that is enough. It is a continual process, and to be honest, if there has been a change in your mate's attitude toward you, it very well could be that the goofy, happy moments have died and the butterflies have been replaced by moths.

Couple Time Moment

Talk to each other about the things that you miss your partner doing or saying—the things that make the person goofy and happy that you may not have noticed you have stopped. Do not assume! Write those things down so you can keep them in your "thought gate" (your mind) and begin doing them again.

Put in the Work

How many of you are willing to put in the work to make your marriage better? No matter how happy you are, marriage is a job. You have to work at it, or it will become stale, and you cannot afford to have a stale marriage. Whatever it takes, you have to put in the work to make the marriage better. What you put into anything will determine what you will get out. Couples have to be mindful in relationships and not view them as one-sided. It is not about how *you* feel or *you* think but how *we* feel and what *we* think. Anytime your relationship is one-sided, it says that someone is not putting in the work. It says that someone has given up. It says that someone thinks he or she does not have to make an effort to keep the butterflies active.

Some couples think that it is in the beginning of the relationship that you put in the most work; however, that is not the case. The older your relationship gets, the more work it requires because changes take place in the relationship as years pass. The goals and dreams are different the older your relationship gets; therefore, you always have to refresh yourself with each other. You will get out what you put in. Do you want a flabby relationship or a strong relationship?

If you want a strong relationship, you have to put in the work.

If you want a flabby relationship, keep doing nothing.

Why Are We Here?

What's up with the constant arguing like we are enemies? What's going on? It is not a question of *who* did something but about *what happened.* You need to get an RCA, a "Root Cause Analysis" of where things went wrong. Sometimes we think that because the issue appears big, it is big. To be honest, it is big because we made it big.

If couples would learn *why* they are arguing and *what* caused them to argue, chances are the root cause of the argument can be addressed and solved. What if the other person said something that you misunderstood? What if you perceived it the wrong way? What if that one word you *thought* you heard was not what was said? We would be surprised that, if we took the time to actually hear each other, we would be able to answer the question "Why are we here?" Do not jump the gun or to conclusions. Ask your mate to clarify what he or she did or said. Let the other person tell you; if you disagree or see that there could possibly be an issue with it, tell him or her. Maybe the other person did not see it the way you did. Maybe he or she did not think about the suggestions you just gave. Men do not think like women and women do not think like men. There really is no right or wrong answer; it is a difference of perception stemming from different points of view.

Do not bring a problem to the table and just slam it down. Bring it by setting it down and finding out the root cause of the problem. It's not what you say but how you say it (slam it or set it down). You should never ask, "Why are we here?" and not have an answer.

How Badly Do You Want It?

How badly do you want your relationship to work? Is it worth your time and effort? Is it worth giving up being right, wanting to be right, insisting that you are right? Is it worth allowing others to bring division into your relationship? Is it worth fighting over and fighting for? Is it worth standing up for? How far do you want your relationship to go? How far do you want your relationship to grow? How important is your relationship to you? How important is your mate to you? Are you willing to listen and accept issues that you do not notice you have? Are you willing to make adjustments if needed? These are questions we should ask ourselves and our mates.

Each relationship is going to have some rough patches. You have to be willing to work through issues. You have to be willing to do what it takes to make your relationship a success. You never want to *force* something to work. You cannot fit a square peg in a round hole. You have to be willing to do and give in the relationship for it to work. *It is not about just you!* Are you willing to give of yourself to make each other happy and make your relationship work?

How badly do you want it? You need to ask yourself this question when you are mad, upset, angry, or hurt. Is what you want for your relationship enough for you to adjust yourself (not your partner), change yourself (not your partner), and correct yourself (not your partner)? If you want something badly enough, you will find yourself doing whatever it takes to make it work.

> Make allowance for each other's faults, and forgive anyone who offends you. Remember, the Lord forgave you, so you must forgive others. Above all, clothe yourselves with love, which binds us all together in perfect harmony.
>
> —Colossians 3:13–14

For the Sisters Only: "HUSH"

Listen, sisters, listen. Stop talking so much and trying to *make* your mate do what you want him to do, go where you want him to go, and be who you want him to be. *You* (somebody shout *You*) have to apply 2 Peter 3:1–2 to your everyday agenda:

> Wives, in the same way submit yourselves to your own husbands so that, if any of them do not believe the word, they may be won over without words by the behavior of their wives, when they see the purity and reverence of your lives.

No one follows the directives of controlling people. Stop that! Act like God has instructed through the act of submission by not saying a word, but acting in purity, reverence, and meekness. When your mate sees you not acting all *extra* but loving him in spite of the way you think is not right, God will show him the truth. Keep in mind that he is responsible and accountable for the household. Let God handle him. You just *hush!*

Just Because

When was the last time you did something without having a reason? Doing something special does not always require a special occasion. Doing something special also does not mean that you have to go out, spend money, or overdo it. Sometimes it is the small things that are priceless.

Have you ever done anything "just because": just because I wanted to… just because I love you…just because it is you. I know you might be thinking that the other person does not need it, or can buy it for himself or herself, or can wait. You do not need an excuse to do something in order to tell your mate you are thinking about him or her; do it "just because."

"Just because" moments rekindle. "Just because" moments reconnect. "Just because" moments rejuvenate. "Just because" moments revive. "Just because" moments restore. "Just because" moments regenerate and "just because" moments reignite the relationship. Do not tell the other person you are doing it…surprise him or her. Do it spontaneously, but, more importantly, do it "just because."

~~~~~~

Then the Lord said to Samuel, "Behold, I am about to do a thing in Israel at which the two ears of everyone who hears it will tingle."

—1 Samuel 3:11 (ESV)

Even God knows how to surprise his people!

The Other Room

In every relationship, arguments will happen and temperatures may rise. It happens even in the best of marriages/relationships; however, it is important to learn how to be what we call "healthy angry." The apostle Paul states it this way: "Be angry and do not sin" (Ephesians 4:26). There is "good anger" (where you have a right to be angry because your mate made a foolish decision that goes against an agreement or decision you made together) and "bad anger" (anger that leads to physical, mental, verbal, and emotional abuse toward each other). Learn how to fight fairly and not cause harm. Do not disrespect each other by calling names, pointing out flaws, degrading, or using profanity, because that is where the sin of your actions begins.

One thing works well for us is when either of us gets angry, the angry one will get up and go to "the other room." The rule is the other one cannot follow. The purpose of leaving the room is to allow a cooling-off period. Calmer heads will always prevail. One of the best ways to work it out is to separate yourself, get yourself together, and think. Going to the other room gets you away, not from the person, but from the situation that caused you to be angry. This allows you time to dissect the situation and think rationally rather than angrily. One thing that is a huge no-no is that you do not leave the house, and divorce is not an option.

The Magic Eraser

If you could magically erase one thing out of your relationship, what would it be? Mr. Clean sells an awesome product called Magic Eraser. This eraser, according to the makers of Mr. Clean products, is made of melamine, which is just an organic base in the form of white crystals. When combined with other compounds, it can transform into a plush foam—the Magic Eraser—with a sandpaper-like microscopic texture. You can use it to scrub off sticky dirt and scum from all kinds of surfaces; however; you have to avoid using it on "delicate or glossy exteriors." My, my, my!

Each person in the relationship will have imperfections. Each person will get on the other's nerves and be an irritant at times. There should be some scrubbing away at nasty attitudes and excessive drama that needs to come to a halt—or literally be erased away. However, you should always look out for the "delicate or glossy exteriors" of each other's internal individuality. Make sure what you want to "magically" erase is not what you really need from that person to keep you straight, to keep you focused, to keep you on track, or to keep you from stumbling and falling. Not everything that seems good to erase is good to erase. Even God loves our flaws; He takes them and calls them beautiful as He pushes us into purpose. Think about it: if we "magically" erased everything we did not like about each other, what would be the next thing we erased when what was left did not satisfy us either? Hmmmm.

> Not that I have already obtained this or am already perfect, but I press on to make it my own, because Christ Jesus has made me his own.
> —Philippians 3:12 (ESV)

Sorry...Are You Really?

One of the biggest issues couple have is apologizing when one feels like he or she is in the right. There is nothing wrong with being right, but there is also nothing wrong with being wrong. If you continue, or have a tendency, to say you are sorry but continue to do, say, or act the same way, at some point your apology will be unbelievable and unacceptable. Why? Because your "sorry" is now viewed like the boy (or girl) who cried wolf. You have said it so much that even you believe it—but are you really sorry? Or are you just saying it so he or she will hush and move on?

When you are truly sorry, you will not let pride get in the way of admitting that you are wrong and it is not your intention to do it again. Why not go a little further and ask your mate to hold you accountable by pointing out the behavior to you if you do or say it again. In addition, you have to promise not to become upset when it happens. It is amazing how we want things to be better but we have an issue with doing better to be better. Every time you do or say something that you do not apologize for, whether warranted or not, you cause your mate to pull back from you. A hurting person can perceive that lack of an apology as evidence the other person does not care. We should never cause, directly or indirectly, our mates to feel, perceive, or translate our non-apology as not caring. Throw away your pride and just apologize...*and* mean it. Do not continue to waste time that you could be using to make up by breaking up. Whew...that was good!

Have My Back; Don't Hold Me Back!

Let me (Clarence) help my sisters out! One of the most important things to a man in a relationship is having his woman as his main supporter. He may have to make decisions that even he does not want to make himself, but that is his role. Someone has to make decisions and the man must make them because God positioned him to do so. Be careful, women: this is not the time to nag; this is the time to have his back. He needs your support and prayers on decisions that affect not just him but the entire relationship and household.

Nagging is a way of holding him back. He does not need you constantly saying to him that it needs to be this way or that way. Okay...he heard you; now let him make the decision. Do not let him get to the point where he is tired of hearing you. What he is looking for from you is someone who will support him in whatever decision he makes—good, bad, or indifferent.

You have to help meet his emotional needs. A part of meeting his emotional needs is having his back. A part of meeting his support need is *not* holding him back from doing what he was created to do: *lead*. If you do not agree with his decision, go to your prayer closet and tell God on him. If God agrees with you, then He will fix it; if not, leave the decision up to your man.

But I want you to understand that Christ is the head (authority over) of every man, and man is the head of woman, and God is the head of Christ.

—1 Corinthians 11:3 (AMP)

He Gets to Choose

Men, it is your day!

That's right! *You get to choose!* Today you get to choose an "us time" day and what the two of you will do. Now, here is the twist: you have to choose something that she likes to do, whether you want to do it or not. It could be playing a game, reading a book together, dancing, singing, shopping…whatever. Now men, this means that if you are not sure, *ask her…do not assume.*

Remember, she could have changed her likes and you will not know if you do not ask.

Have fun with each other!

Still an Individual

As much as you love doing things together, going places together, and spending time together, you still are individuals. We do not always like the same things. We have some things that we both like, some things we both do not like, and some things one likes and the other does not like.

There is a plan designed for each of you that requires your individuality at times. There needs to be understanding of each other's dreams, visions, and goals. You should be the first cheerleader, first supporter, first one praying, and the first one standing by the other's side when he or she succeeds. Sometimes we do not realize how important it is to spend time doing things that we enjoy because we may feel like it is a "rule" to always do things together.

Neither of you should be offended nor should it make you feel loved any differently in your individuality. This is healthy and necessary for both of you. Just remember to support each other in your individuality. Remember, you are not just a wife/husband/boyfriend/girlfriend; you are also a woman/man/mother/father/sister/brother/daughter/son/best friend/minister/supervisor/ employee and so much more.

With those many titles, you need to be able to have some self-care and self-enjoyment every now and then.

Do not make the other person feel that because he or she wants to do something without you that he or she is wrong. The other person is not wrong; he or she is still an individual while being one with you.

She Needs, He Needs

It is important to recognize each other's needs. If we are honest, we think we know what each other needs. In many cases, we do not know what the other needs because our design is different. God has designed us differently as male and female. We neither think the same nor respond the same. We are not supposed to, but we are supposed to know what the other needs. Men, she does not need you saying no to everything. She needs to hear from you how proud you are of her and how what she does makes a difference in the family and in you.

Encourage her to dream and follow those dreams. She needs to hear that you will protect her and be her security. She needs to know that you will provide not only things but moral, emotional, and spiritual support for her wellbeing. She needs you to recognize that, although you are a couple, you are also individuals. She needs intimacy, not just sex.

When was the last time you held her hand, sang her a song on one knee, made her smile from doing something goofy, or hold her. Her number one need is *emotional* need. If you give her that, she will give you her.

She Needs, He Needs (continued)

In every relationship, men have two needs: physical and emotional. Intimacy through talking and holding hands is not what men need. You show him how much he is loved by meeting his physical needs. God created the woman for the man, the man knows that, and he treasures that gift to him from God. He needs to know he is doing his best job by you telling him he is doing a great job. He needs praise from you. If he is providing, covering, keeping, and protecting you, he needs to know.

A lot of men feel that they do a lot of things with no recognition. He needs your approval of what he has done. In other words, stroke his ego. He will take great care of you if you will take care of his physical and emotional needs.

How do you balance each other's needs? You have to be honest and upfront with each other about what you need. Stop trying to change him. Stop trying to change her. Do not make the mistake of just focusing on your needs and not the other's needs. That is selfish and God did not create us to be selfish.

Tell each other what you need. If it is something the other person would like to do or try, hear him or her out. Needs change. What he or she needed five years ago, he or she may not need now. You need to know that because it is important to address each other's needs.

Don't Hide It

One of the greatest things you can do in a relationship is to keep an open communication flow. Now, let us be honest: all communication is not the best, but it is necessary. Men, you have to keep in mind that her makeup is that of meeting the need. Ladies, you have to keep in mind that his makeup is that of providing for the need. Therefore, each one needs the other. Since you need each other, you have to be open with each other. Do not hide your feelings or thoughts on an issue.

One of the things that will destroy a relationship is having hidden stuff. The last thing you want is for your mate to hide things from you. He or she has a right to know. Everything that affects you affects your mate. Even if it seems small to you, do not hide it. Talk about finances, talk about your job, talk about your health, talk about the children, talk about how what makes you angry.

Things that are critical to your life and your relationship need to be made known, not hidden. If you hide things, your marriage will be an excuse not an enlargement. No excuses will be necessary if you do not hide things from one another.

Not only do you not need to hide *things*, but do not hide how you feel. It is your voice. Open up to each other with understanding, care, and concern. If you hide your feelings, bigger problems will come because you did not use your voice. Luke 8:17 says, "For all that is secret will eventually be brought into the open, and everything that is concealed will be brought to light and made known to all."

Couples, stop hiding what is inside. Be honest with your mate and yourself. Mate, listen—you just might learn something that you did not know.

Outside Help

Tradition has taught us that talking with someone (e.g., a mediator, a counselor, a trusted, wise person, or a strong couple you trust to serve as marriage mentors) is that it is only for "crazy people who are dysfunctional." Well, guess what couples? We all need help, we all have crazy moments, and we all have some type of dysfunction around and in us.

Most of the time when we handle conflict, we spend the time pointing fingers at the other person. How can you handle conflict when you are a part of the conflict? Now that is dysfunctional thinking. It is okay to get help. We have to stop painting this beautiful picture that we are good, when in reality we are not good. Conflict will present itself in the relationship and if you are unable to resolve it among yourselves, it is good to get outside help. Outside help is good because it is *outside*. Outside help does not have a clue of what is going on in your relationship. Outside help is neutral and takes no sides. Outside help will assist in getting inside peace.

Just talk to someone you trust. Make sure he or she can hold water. There are some great outside helpers who can help.

Does it Really Matter?

There are times as couples that we pay too much attention to petty stuff. We have to say to ourselves, *This is petty; does it really matter?* It has no benefit to your relationship at all, so is it worth breaking the peace, breaking apart from each other, or breaking up? Does it really matter if you win the argument? Does it really matter if the toilet paper rolls over or under? Does it really matter if the toothpaste is squeezed from the bottom, middle, or top? Does it matter if the toilet seat is left up or down? Does it matter if the towels are single-folded or double-folded? Think about it. Does it really matter?

We need to look at things based on the importance to us as a couple because the things that do not matter does not gain us anything. If you are not careful, you will find yourself arguing about stuff that seriously does not matter. That falls into the category called *pettiness*. Pettiness can go both ways. When things get petty, you stop progressing because the pettiness becomes the center of discussion and attention. Galatians 5:22–23 says, "But the fruit of the Spirit is love, joy, peace, forbearance, kindness, goodness, faithfulness, gentleness and self-control"—*not* pettiness! Do not let your relationship be based on pettiness but instead focus on what really does matter: each other.

Stop That!

"Hey…let me tell you about my day! It was actually very interesting because I saw—"

"Do you like the way this looks?"

"Yes, it looks nice, but let me tell you what I saw today! When I was going—"

"What do you want to eat for dinner?"

"I haven't really thought about it, but what I was trying to say was—"

"I think I want some seafood because I haven't had any in a while."

The room is now silent. No talking—just staring.

"What? Why are you looking at me like that?"

Continued stare.

"Why are you staring at me?"

Continued stare.

"What is wrong with you?" Suddenly, without a warning, you hear this.

"You are so rude! That was so disrespectful! I was trying to share something with you and you kept cutting me off! I am tired of you thinking that what I say is not important or acting as if you do not want to be bothered or I am boring you! But…that's okay. You don't have to worry about me trying to share anything with you again!"

Sound familiar? That's okay, you do not have to raise your hand. Couples, *stop that!* Stop interrupting. Stop turning the other person's voice away. Stop disrespecting. Stop shutting your ears while looking the other person dead in the face. Failure to communicate and failure to listen equals a failure to meet each other's needs. Did he or she bother you with talking when you met? Of course not! You talked and the other person listened. The other person talked and you listened. Then you giggled and grinned at each other for hours. What happened to those moments?

Don't Mess up a Good Thing

Let me (Demetria), help my brothers out! I thank God that He has given you the role of head, leader, priest of the house, chief, and patriarch. It fits you well. As a woman, I would not want to be in your shoes because the responsibility and accountability that has been placed on you by God is heavy, which brings me to this point. You have a weight that can be great. You have to make tough, unpopular decisions at times, and I commend you for doing your best to make sure things are in order.

I want to give you a spiritual nugget to always carry with you while you are in your role. Proverbs 18:22 says this: "He who finds a wife finds a good thing and obtains favor from God" (KJV). Another translation says, "The man who finds a wife finds a treasure and receives favor from the Lord" (AMP). I simply want to share this: your good thing and treasure is in your mate that *you*, not someone else, found. In finding her *you* have received *favor* from God. She is the releaser of the favor for you when you found her.

Brothers, as much as you have been assigned a very important role, do not mess up the favor of your "good thing." She benefits from your role and you benefit from finding her. She was not created from your head so you could play mind games with her; she was not created from your feet so you could walk over her and treat her as number two when she should always be number one. She was created from your rib, which was taken from your side, right next to your heart, to walk beside you as you love each other.

She will not always get it right, but she has in her what you need. If she does not do right, go tell God on her.

Ride Until the Wheels Fall Off...Then What?

The urban adage, "I'll ride with you until the wheels fall off" sounds like the unity covenant of someone who will be there right by your side—until something comes along and messes everything up. According to the Urban Dictionary, it means "to keep something going as long as you possibly can, the way you would drive a car until the wheels fall off."

As we thought about this adage a question crossed our minds: "What is the next step after the wheels fall off?" In other words, your relationship is going great, things are peaceful and then suddenly all types of wrong breaks loose! Financial issues, health issues, job loss, family divisions, and on and on. So what just happened? The wheels fell off. Now what?

One of the things that we sometimes forget is a three letter word called *vow*. "I, (Name), take you, (Name), to be my wife/husband, to have and to hold from this day forward, for better, for worse, for richer, for poorer, in sickness and in health, to love and to cherish, till death do us part." Maybe you are not married but you have made a vow that you are exclusively dating one person. A vow is a solemn promise.

Whatever the relationship, your promise is your bond. Just as you should not walk away when things get tough in life, you do not get out of the car when the wheels fall off. Instead, you sit there in that broken down car together, call a tow truck, have it transported to the tire shop, buy another set, and ride on your new wheels. One thing you should "never" do is get out of the car (call your friend, family, Uber or Lyft) to come and get you and leave your mate.

Do not leave each other when it gets tough; get tough and keep riding… together.

Gentlemen Only

Men, let me just be real with you. There are some things you need to let go of and respond, "Okay." Period. Trust me—you are not going to win every battle. What is important is to establish some relationship rules to help when "Okay" seems hard. When you have a tendency to always be right and make it about you, you are actually breaking her heart. It is not about you being right; it is about being right in the relationship with her.

"Okay" is a winning word, a manly word, a smart word, and a "leave it alone bruh, you are not going to win this one" word. When you use it, you both win.

Ready...Set...Goals!

Goals are set to bring forth a desired result. When we set goals, we say, "This is what I desire to come forth in my life and I am willing to press, stretch, and reach toward that goal." We become motivated, on fire, and ready to conquer whatever challenge gets in our way. But what about in our relationship? Do we have goals for our relationship? Do we have at least one set of goals? No? Why not?

When was the last time you sat down and talked seriously about a goal (a desired result) in your relationship? What do you want to accomplish together? Where do you want to go together? When do you want to start working on the goal together? Have you ever thought about the fact that the reason why you may still be doing or saying the same thing but wanting different results is because you haven't set goals?

Today, let us help you out. Here is your homework assignment. 1) Sit down with each other without interruption. 2) Set one goal that the two of you will work toward the next four months. 3) Set one more goal that you both will work toward the next four months. 4) Finally, set one goal that you both will work toward for the last four months. That is a total of one year with three goals (desired results) that you will work on together. It does not matter what the goals are as long as you *both* want them and you commit to working on them together. Write them below; when you accomplish them, write more.

Your relationship should not only include your individual goals but your together goals as well.

Goal 1: _____

Goal 2: _____

Goal 3: _____

Let Me Tell You

There are many fun games to play: board games, electronic games, video games, card games, dancing games, or made-up games. Fun, Fun, Fun! However, one game that is cool to play when you are just having fun, but not okay when it comes to your relationship, is the Guessing Game. Ladies, it irritates men when they have to guess. They are logical thinkers and they are not trying to spend all day and night guessing. That is not a fun game to them. Just tell them. Men, it is hurtful to her when she does finally tell and you dismiss it (whatever the "it" is) like it is not important, as if to say, "You will get over it." Why are you hiding your feelings and thoughts from each other? Seriously. Why? What is it about his or her reaction that makes you feel you cannot tell the other person how you feel, what you are thinking, and what are your dreams?

There is a serious problem when the one you love and care about cannot tell you *anything*. That is a problem. Why? Because the first person your mate should be able to tell anything to is *you*. Now let's be real and set the record straight. Not every person who feels like he or she is not being listened to runs into the arms of another person. However, the person will run to seclusion, depression, loneliness, and hardness of the heart. Those things are worse than another person. Watch the behavior of your mate when he or she shuts down on you. You think he or she has an attitude? Oh no, he or she has been trying to tell you something.

She Gets to Choose

Ladies, it is your day!

That's right. *You get to choose!* Today you get to choose an "us time" day and what the two of you will do. Now, here is the twist: you have to choose something that he likes to do whether you want to do it or not. It could be watch sports all day, cook his favorite meal, rub his feet, cut the grass... whatever. Now ladies, this means that if you are not sure, *ask him. Do not assume.*

Remember, he could have changed his likes and you will not know if you do not ask.

Have fun with each other!

Bring Back the SPICE

Sometimes, your relationship will start to turn a little dull or start to show some wear and tear. What has happened is that the spice is gone. The excitement is gone. Remember, when you first met each other, no one could separate you. Your eyes were glued to each other. On your wedding day, you were excited and looking good. Now the excitement is gone and you need to find out why.

One thing that we recommend to bring back the spice is to do something to commemorate your wedding day or your date day (day of your first date). For instance, we married on June 23, so each month on the twenty-third, we celebrate our day with dinner, spending time together, and so on. Sometimes we do nothing but talk. We also set aside an agreed time once per week, which is every Wednesday, that we call "us time." No phones, computers, work, ministry work, or sorority work are allowed. We use us time for us. Think about something memorable that keeps the flavor in your relationship.

Spontaneous Practice Initiating Couples' Enjoyment (SPICE)—that's right—SPICE it up! Wherever there is lack, bring it back. Bring sexy back. Put Luther Vandross on, press Barry White on the playlist, Usher in Usher, dance to Major singing "This is Why I Love You," and don't leave out India Arie with "Steady Love."

Spices are used to enhance the flavor. Enhance each other, couples, enhance!

Stay in Your Lane

Changes will take place. You should not still be in the same lane (place) that you were in last year as a couple. There should always be goals, visions, dreams, and plans that you have for your relationship. All of those require change. Your likes and dislikes have changed. Let your mate know about your changes. Let him or her know your favorite color has changed, your style has changed, your wants have changed, and your needs have changed. Change will change. You cannot stay in the same lane all the way to your destination, because chances are a fork in the road is going to pop up in the middle of your lane. You are going to have to detour from that lane at some time in your life.

Change is healthy and it is okay because it says there is growth. You have to adjust, and not just this year, but in years to come. Clarence likes the temperature hot. Demetria likes it cold. It was opposite ten years ago. Each of us had to make an adjustment because if we did not, our marriage would either freeze or burn up. Your lane will change; but you also have to stay there until it is time to change again. Do not try to change for someone else or require him or her to change for you. Do not try to put your foot down because you want to control him or her.

Have an understanding that if I stay in my lane, my ride in this relationship will go smoother. There is a place called Lovers' Lane, where lovers would go and hang out for intimate purposes (yeah, that's a more proper choice of words for it). In all seriousness, each one of us needs to have a Lovers' Lane where we stay and ride with each other until the wheels fall off. Then we buy a new set and keep riding.

Thank you all for your love, prayers, and support. It is our prayer that God will touch, grow, and manifest His will in our marriages like never before. We dedicate this devotional to all young couples. Please understand that relationships take work. Put in the work. Be committed to the work. Do your part in the work.
Clarence and Demetria/"Team High"

IT IS WORTH

THE WORK

Printed in the United States
by Baker & Taylor Publisher Services